· ADOLF DEHN DRAWINGS ·

" The very act of drawing made me participate in the life around me."

· ADOLF DEHN DRAWINGS ·

SELECTED BY VIRGINIA DEHN · INTRODUCTION BY CARL ZIGROSSER

UNIVERSITY OF MISSOURI PRESS · COLUMBIA · 1971

STANDARD BOOK NUMBER ISBN 0-8262-0100-8   LIBRARY OF CONGRESS CARD NUMBER 71-134016

COPYRIGHT © 1971 BY THE CURATORS OF THE UNIVERSITY OF MISSOURI

UNIVERSITY OF MISSOURI PRESS, COLUMBIA, MISSOURI 65201   PRINTED AND BOUND IN THE UNITED STATES OF AMERICA

ALL RIGHTS RESERVED

With the exception of those so identified in the captions, the originals of the drawings reproduced in this book are the property of Virginia Dehn. Photographs of the artist are by the following photographers: Herbert Gehr (page 15), Gene Pyle (page 45), Ed Sullivan (page 63 and cover), Roy Stevens (page 89), John D. Schiff (page 141), and William A. Smith (page 163).

INTRODUCTION

There are occasionally artists who exist independently of schools or currents dominant in their time—an independence, whether of technique or philosophy. There are also artists whose work appears to conform but actually does not.

Adolf Dehn was such a man—a practicing artist who developed largely on his own, then ranged widely through basically graphic forms. Although his career included brief periods of employment as a teacher, he was not essentially a teacher and showed no particular concern that he should be followed or not. Very probably, the idea never occurred to him, since his understanding of what he was about as an artist was so intimately concerned with his own life that I doubt he would have felt it possible to explain himself in terms that would have meant anything to the student. He was truly an independent artist, who worked as he saw fit. If others did what he happened to be doing, fine. But he felt no need to follow vogue and occasionally spoke with more than a little acid of those he felt were doing so.

I do not remember how I first met Adolf. It might have been that Boardman Robinson introduced him, but I am more inclined to believe that he just wandered into our gallery—as did other artists—to see shows or buy art books. I had opened the Weyhe Gallery in the fall of 1920 with an exhibition of lithographs by Daumier, and the exhibition had attracted considerable attention. Other artists were bringing in drawings to show to me, and Adolf may have been one of them. At any rate, I liked his work when I saw it, and we managed to sell a few of his drawings. We also encouraged him to make a few lithographs, and our outright purchase of a batch of his drawings made it possible for him to get to Europe at a crucial time in his life.

As I got to know Adolf better and as his personal style ripened into maturity, I came to the conclusion that the mainspring of his art was his experience of living and that technique was secondary. When inspiration failed he sometimes resorted to technical tricks that he used with tongue in cheek, but life always came first. As he once wrote in a letter: "My attitude to life is rather sensuous—and sensual too—and only after I have filled myself with sensuous experiences can I go about working. Putting it simply: when I am fed up, I work. I am crazy about life and want to have as much out of it as I can. Take away my work and I lose interest in life, yet the work comes after my living life, or rather out of it."

From his father, who was a trapper and fisherman, Adolf absorbed some instinctive attitudes—independence, for instance—and especially a habit of looking at the "nature of things." I once charged Dehn with being influenced by Oriental art because I felt there was a similarity of approach between some of his work and Chinese landscape painting and drawing. He denied ever having consciously studied Chinese art. The similarity must therefore have been a shared approach in such matters as "feeling into" the subject or looking at the nature of things.

Obviously, one concerned with the true nature of things is not concerned with the explicit, and Adolf was not. As far as I know, he did not make finished drawings from nature. He doodled a great deal and made many sketches, but they were not what he considered finished drawings. He later would elaborate the sketches and notes into finished drawings in the studio. This was the nature of things in contemplation, the second or real life that he gave to his subject, once he had absorbed and mulled the truth of its being. In a letter from Paris in March, 1928, he wrote: "The dominant passion of my artistic life is to draw, I guess. Landscape ? I shall always do many landscapes, and there is landscape in the Bois de Boulogne, along the Seine and along Rue Vercingetorix, as well as in the Swiss Alps or in Brittany, where I was last summer. I have, in passing, enough notes from my three or four weeks in Brittany to do landscapes all winter, for I do not ~~work from~~ [crossed out by Dehn] do finished things from nature."

"I do not do finished things from nature." How revealing that statement is. His aim never was to produce a mirror-image of nature but to make a picture grow organically. I summed up the process in an earlier essay on Dehn: "In working out a particular problem, he does not start with a rigid conception in mind: he has an intuition about a subject, he feels his way into it. He lets the picture, as elusive as life, grow before his eyes; he does not know the ultimate end, but he knows when it comes to life, when it clicks or is in tune. He works for days and nights when the spell is on him."

Dehn's lithographs have an unusual sense of spontaneity. The spontaneity actually is an absence of fear. Most artists (especially at the beginning) freeze up before the blank stone surface, because a line once applied to the stone can be erased only with great difficulty. There is little difference between Adolf's drawings on stone and his drawing on paper. They are all "drawings." All the methods and devices he employed on stone he also employed on paper. Even scratching and gouging: there are a number of drawings on paper treated in that way.

I should say a word here about the considerable number of caricatures—many of them social in nature—that Dehn did. In this decade, his seeming pre-occupation with such subjects could easily be misread. He did not develop his talents as a caricaturist to implement a deep commitment to social change. He was primarily an artist, not a propagandist or revolutionary activist, despite his radical leanings and his contribution of drawings to *The New Masses* and other such publications. In this respect, Boardman Robinson was his teacher and his model; both were artists, not propagandists.

A letter written from Paris on May 9, 1928, is illuminating regarding Dehn's idea of caricature: "However, I don't understand Robinson's remark, 'caricaturing nature' or your explanation of his remark [in my explanation I equated "to caricature" with "to lack respect for"]—your explanation may be true, but it has nothing to do with caricature; such statements as 'lack of solid observation', 'too little sense of reality', all these may be good criticism of my work, but not a definition of the word caricature. I do not think I caricature nature. I might if I could, but I can't—at least I don't think I caricature nature any more than Robinson does. But we are merely arguing over a definition." [Dehn was holding to a very strict definition of caricature.] I should note that Dehn—even after his later success as a landscapist—held that his satiric work was of equal, if not of paramount, importance. We may not judge it so today, but we *must* not judge it in terms of social significance; it is commentary by a man whose first concern was his art.

In sum, Dehn was par excellence a graphic social commentator of integrity and, later, a landscape watercolorist. His contribution, indeed his significance, is that he was an independent, honest man. His two dominant themes—nature and human nature—are everywhere evident in his work. His variations on the themes are near endless, and all were executed with great facility.

I would hope that this book of his drawings will show this man in the dimensions of those variations.

Carl Zigrosser

Philadelphia, Pennsylvania

July, 1970

CHRONOLOGY

(1895–1968)

November 22, 1895 Born at Waterville, Minnesota; parents, Arthur Clark Dehn and Emilie Haase Dehn. **Spring 1914** Valedictorian, graduating class Waterville High School. **September 1914–1917** Studied at Minneapolis Art Institute. **Spring 1917** First drawing published—*The Masses.* **Fall 1917** Won scholarship to Art Students League, New York. **1918** Spent four months in camp, Spartanburg, South Carolina, as conscientious objector to war. **Armistice 1918** Volunteered for nonmilitary duty at a reconstruction hospital, Asheville, North Carolina, teaching drawing and painting to tubercular soldiers for eight months. **1919** Returned to New York. **1920** Made first lithograph. **1921** First exhibited drawing purchased by Arthur B. Davies; first trip to Europe, settling in Vienna for two-and-a-half years. **1923** First one-man show, Weyhe Gallery, New York. **1920's** Drawings published in *The Dial, Liberator, Broom, Jugend, Querschnitt.* **1926** Married Mura Ziperovitch, Vienna; London, series of drawings of Welsh miners published in London *Daily Herald.* **1928** Paris, produced 75 lithographs, working at Atelier Desjobert. **Spring 1929** Returned to America. **1931–1932** Paris, lithography at Atelier Desjobert. **1933** Returned to America. **1935, 1939, 1940** One-man exhibitions at Weyhe Gallery. **Summer–Fall 1936** Spent in Europe, chiefly Austria and Yugoslavia. **Spring 1938** First one-man show of watercolors, Weyhe Gallery. **1938–1939** Taught summer school, Stephens College, Columbia, Missouri. **1939** Awarded Guggenheim fellowship; traveled to many parts of United States and Mexico. **Summers 1940, 1941, 1942** Taught at Colorado Springs Fine Arts Center. **1941** Joined Associated American Artists Gallery. **1943** Citation from United States Treasury: "Distinguished service rendered in behalf of War Savings Program." **1945** Traveled to Venezuela, one-man exhibition in Caracas; published *Watercolor Painting*, Studio Publications. **November 1947** Married Virginia Engleman. **Winter 1948** Key West, Florida. **January, February, March, 1949** Lived and worked in Haiti. **1950** Published *How to Draw and Print Lithographs*, Lawrence Barrett, coauthor, for American Artists Group, publisher. **Winter 1951** Taught at Norton Museum School, West Palm Beach, Florida. **March 1951** Trip to Cuba. **1951** Awarded second Guggenheim fellowship. **Winter 1955** Visit to Yucatán and Guatemala. **Summer 1955** Guest of Yaddo Foundation, Saratoga Springs, New York; published *Watercolor Gouache and Casein Painting*, Studio Publication, Thomas Y. Crowell Co. **1957** Joined the Milch Gallery, New York. **February 1958** Retrospective exhibition, "Thirty Years of Lithography," Krasner Gallery, New York. **1958** Eight months' tour to France, Italy, Greece, Turkey, Iran, Lebanon, Afghanistan, India, Kashmir. **1961** Elected Full Academician, National Academy of Design. **1961, 1963, 1965, 1967** Paris, at work on lithography at Atelier Desjobert. **1965** Elected to membership in National Institute of Arts and Letters. **November, December, January, 1965** Visit to Egypt, Ethiopia, Kenya, Guinea, Morocco, Portugal. **Winter 1968** Retrospective exhibitions: FAR Gallery and The Century Association, New York. **May 1968** Died after complications following heart attack, New York City. **1969–1970** Retrospective museum tour organized by The Columbus Gallery of Fine Arts. **1970** Estate represented by the Kennedy Galleries, New York.

CONTENTS

I

CAFÉ SCENES

"The very act of drawing made me participate in the life around me."

1. Artistes' Café. Ink, 12 × 17½, 1923

Adolph Dehn 1923.

2. Café Moment. Ink, 10 × 17, 1923

Adolph Dehn 1923.

3. Jazz and Gilded Cupids Reign. Ink, $14\frac{1}{2} \times 18$, 1923

Adolph Dehn '23. Wien.

4. "Kaffeehaus Konigen." Ink, 12 × 10, 1922

5. Cabaret Entertainer. Ink, $13\frac{3}{4} \times 15$, 1923

Adolph Dehn '23.

6. After Midnight in Most Any Coffeehaus. Ink, 12 × 17½, 1923

7. "The Politicians' Café." Ink, $12\frac{1}{4} \times 17\frac{1}{2}$, 1923

"The Politician's Cafe".

8. "Volks Cafe-house." Ink, $13\frac{1}{2} \times 19$, 1923

9. Dome Terrace. Ink, $12\frac{1}{4} \times 18\frac{1}{2}$, 1920's
Mrs. George Rinker, Jr.

Dome Terrace.   adolf Dehn.

10. Café Ennui. Ink, 15 × 19½, 1924

Adolph Dehn '24.

11. Bistro. Ink, $8\frac{1}{2} \times 13$, 1928

12. Afternoon Hour. Ink, $13\frac{3}{4} \times 18\frac{1}{2}$, 1922

13. Three Men and a Girl. Ink, 8 × 11, 1931

adolf Dehn 1931.

14. Waiting at the Café. Ink plus watercolor wash, $10\frac{1}{2} \times 15$, 1920's

II

JAZZ

"My attitude to life is rather sensuous—and sensual too—and only after I have filled myself with sensuous experiences can I go about working. Putting it simply: when I am fed up, I work. I am crazy about life and want to have as much out of it as I can. Take away my work and I lose interest in life, yet the work comes after my living life, or rather out of it."

15. Jazz Band. Ink, $13\frac{1}{2} \times 19\frac{1}{2}$, 1929

Adolf Dehn 1929.

16. The Clam House. Ink, $14\frac{1}{2} \times 22$, 1930

Adolf Dehn 1930.
"The Club House"

17. Night at the Savoy. Ink, $14\frac{1}{4} \times 21$, 1930's

18. Jazz in Wien. Ink, $12\frac{1}{4} \times 17\frac{1}{2}$, 1926

19. Jazz Dancer. Ink, 10 × 7¾, 1929

20. Jazz Babies. Ink, $13\frac{1}{2} \times 19$, 1927

Adolf Dehn 1927

21. "That's Jazz." Ink, 14 × 18½, 1929

22. Rooftop Party. Ink, 14 × 21½, 1930

III

PARK SCENES

"... ever since the collapse of the Victorian concept of life, there has been an intense, often painful search in all the fields of art for new and better standards. During these past few years of chaos and confusion this has been particularly marked. Dissatisfied with artificial religious, political, moral and aesthetic notions and filled with the bravery of a man who has little he cares to cling to, the artist set out to look anew at his world."

23. Dog Days. Ink, $11\frac{3}{4} \times 17$, 1924

adolph Dehn '24. dry.   Dog Days.

24. Fine Day. Ink, $14\frac{1}{4} \times 18\frac{1}{2}$, 1924

Adolph Dehn 1924.

Fine Day.

25. Hyde Park, London. Ink, $14\frac{1}{2} \times 20\frac{1}{4}$, 1926

26. Sunday Stroll, Vienna. Pen, brush, and ink, $12\frac{1}{4} \times 19$, 1927
The Museum of Modern Art, New York

Adolf Dehn 1927.

27. Old People in the Park. Ink, $12\frac{7}{8} \times 20$, 1927

adolf Dehn 1927.

28. St. Francis in Central Park. Ink, $14\frac{1}{2} \times 22$, 1952

Adolf Dehn 52

29. The Seals in Central Park. Ink, 13 × 18¾, 1929

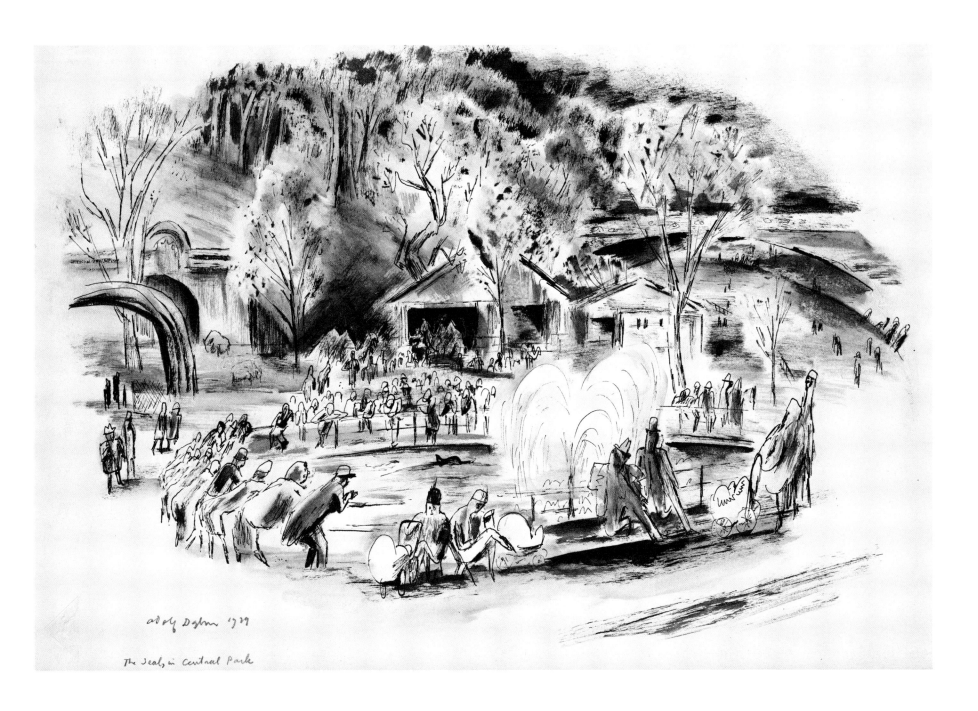

adof Dehn 1939

The Seal, in Central Park

30. ''Au Sacre du Printemps.'' Ink, $13\frac{1}{2} \times 19$, 1926

"Au Sacre de Printemps"

adolf Dehn '26.

31. In the Luxembourg. Ink, 14 × 17, 1924

Adolph Dehn 1924.   Berthe Luxemburg.

32. Stadt Park, Wien. Ink, $14 \times 20\frac{1}{2}$, 1923

Adolph Dehn 1923.
Stadt Park Wien.

33. Park People. Ink, 13 × 17½, 1924

34. Sunny Afternoon. Ink, 13 × 17, 1920's

Adolph Dehn.

IV

LIFE IN GENERAL

"Social criticism and caricature, I like to do that sort of drawing, although
I feel the words, social criticism, are too serious. Preposterous things
are about me; I comment on them, that's all."

35. Yvonne Dubois. Ink, 19 × 15½, *c.* 1928

"Yvonne Dubois"

36. My Good Friend, Emil Ganso, at Work. Ink, 12 × 16, 1940's

37. Inhibited Gentleman. Ink, 11 × 18, 1930

38. After Lunch. Ink, 10 × 12½, 1930's

39. Man with Cane #1. Ink, $10\frac{1}{2} \times 8$, 1926
40. Man with Cane #2. Ink, $11\frac{1}{2} \times 7$, c. 1926

41. Instructive Walk. Ink, $11\frac{1}{2} \times 16\frac{1}{2}$, 1920's

42. Physical Fitness. Ink, 8 × 14, 1925

Wolf Dehn '25

43. Landstrasse, Wien. Ink, 10 × 17½, 1923

Adolph Dehn. 23.

Landstrasse Wien.

44. Pension in Vienna. Ink, $13\frac{1}{2} \times 17\frac{1}{2}$, 1920's

adolph Dehn

45. Frau Rabinovitch und Frau Ziperovitch. Ink, 12 × 13, 1925

Frau Rabinovitch und Frau Ziperovitch.   Adolf Dehn '25

46. Stefansplatz, Wien. Ink, $11\frac{1}{2} \times 15\frac{1}{2}$, 1925

47. Subway. Ink and watercolor wash, 7¼ × 12, 1925

adolph Dehn '25.

Subway.

48. Untitled Drawing. Ink, 15 × 22, 1920's
Mr. and Mrs. Louis Farber

49. "All for a Piece of Meat." Ink, $7\frac{1}{2} \times 11\frac{1}{2}$, 1927
Philadelphia Museum of Art

Adolf Dehn 1927.

50. Fur Coats. Ink, $12\frac{1}{2} \times 20$, 1947

51. The Wise and Foolish Virgins. Ink, 13 × 20, 1927

adolf Dehn 1927.

52. Shop on Fourteenth Street. Ink, $11\frac{1}{2} \times 18$, 1929

53. Easter Parade, Fifth Avenue. Conte crayon, 17 × 23, 1940

adolf Dehn 1940
Easter Parade – Fifth Ave.

54. Runway. Ink, 14 × 19, *c.* 1929–1930

55. Chorus Girls. Ink, $12\frac{7}{8} \times 17\frac{1}{4}$, 1947

56. "She said, that you said, that I said, that they said." Ink, 16 × 22½, 1947

57. Umbrellas in the Rain. Brush and ink, $13\frac{1}{4} \times 18\frac{3}{4}$, 1920's

58. Lohengrin. Ink, 13 × 19, 1926

Lohengrin.

Adolf Dehn 1926.

59. Clowns. Ink, 12 × 17, 1928

60. Mayan Women. Ink wash, $25\frac{1}{2} \times 19\frac{1}{2}$, 1955

V

SKETCH BOOK

How can it [camera] compare to sketching, when in the very act of drawing I am
able to feel at one with my subject? The life around me becomes my own as I
draw. In turn I give my own subjective interpretation to my scene."

61. Sketch Book Page. Crayon, 12½ × 15, 1940's

62. Kabul, Afghanistan Sketch Book. Pencil, $10\frac{5}{8} \times 13\frac{7}{8}$, 1958

Turban
Sahr

purple

pink

girl —
dochtar

Faded
Blue

green tan

tan

AD. June 16
1958
Kabul.

63. Kuchi Tents, Afghanistan Sketch Book. Pencil, $10\frac{5}{8} \times 13\frac{7}{8}$, 1958

Kuchi Kamp.

Tents, rich brown sepia
patched against bright gravel light
sandy beige.

— Black.

— red
red.

Tent — chaïma

A.D. Sunday June 58. Kuchi Tents,

64. Page from Sketch Book. Pencil, $7\frac{7}{8} \times 9\frac{3}{4}$, 1942

65. Pelouse Interdite. Pencil, 10 × 12½, 1960's

66. Café Tabletop Doodles. Ink, 10 × 11, 1960's

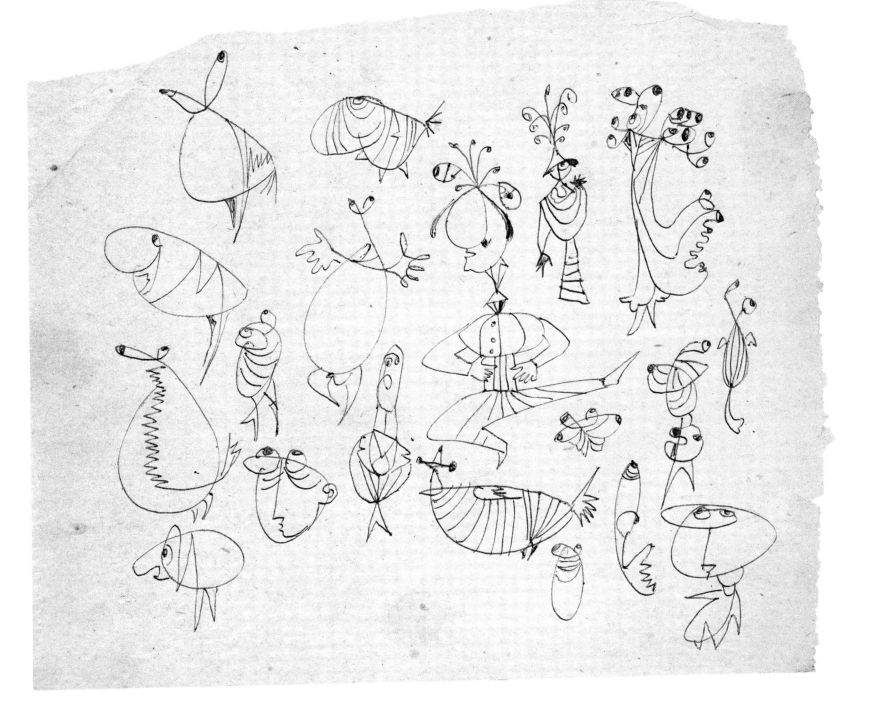

67. Croix de Mission, Haiti. Pencil, $13\frac{3}{4} \times 16\frac{3}{4}$, 1949

Croix de Mission, Haiti

68. Page from Central Park Sketch Book. Pencil, $11\frac{3}{4} \times 17\frac{5}{8}$, 1957

69. Nuns Painting. Litho crayon, $14\frac{1}{2} \times 19$, 1940's

70. The Ohio River from Park. Ink, 14 × 16½, 1964

Haze over distance
green grey blue

AD May 30, 1984
The Ohio River from   Park

VI

CITY AND LANDSCAPES

"When the eye, the heart and the brain, and the hand merge into a spontaneous gesture, you have drawing."

71. Park in May. Ink, 16 × 20, 1920's

72. Church in Valley of the Chevreuse. Crayon and ink, $14\frac{1}{2} \times 19\frac{1}{2}$, 1928

Adolf Dehn 1928

73. The Bridge at Moret-sur-Loing. Ink, $12\frac{3}{4} \times 19\frac{3}{4}$, 1928

Für Murka!
Octobre 7, 1928
Dufin.

The Bridge at Mont sur Loing.

74. Waterville, Minnesota. Ink and crayon, $14\frac{1}{2} \times 16\frac{1}{2}$, 1920's

Adolph Dehn
Waterville, Minn.

75. Landscape with House. Ink, $13\frac{3}{4} \times 20\frac{1}{4}$, 1920's

76. Speed Limit 8 Miles per Hour. Ink wash, 14 × 21, 1931

SPEED LIMIT
8 MILES
PER HOUR

77. Landscape. Ink wash, 15 × 22, *c.* 1930's

Adolf Dehn

78. Cemetery. Ink wash, 15 × 22, 1930

79. On Eighth Avenue. Ink wash, $14\frac{1}{2} \times 22$, 1929

80. New York Night. Ink, 15 × 22, 1930
Mr. and Mrs. John S. McCombe

New York Night.   adolf Dehn 09

81. New York Skyline from Brooklyn. Ink wash, 14 × 21, 1931

82. Lake George. Ink wash, $13 \times 19\frac{1}{2}$, c. 1955

adolf Dehn.

83. Yaddo Woods. Ink wash, 14 × 21, 1955

adolf Dehn

84. Duck Shooting. Brush and wash, $12\frac{3}{8} \times 19\frac{1}{2}$, 1932
Mr. Carl Zigrosser

85. Hill in Spring. Ink, $14\frac{1}{4} \times 19\frac{1}{2}$, 1928
Philadelphia Museum of Art

86. Hillside. Ink, lampblack, wash, $19\frac{3}{4} \times 29\frac{1}{2}$, 1960
Norfolk Museum of Arts and Sciences

adolf Dehn

87. Tuscan Landscape. Ink wash, 16 × 22, 1961

88. Mountain Landscape. Ink wash, $20\frac{1}{4} \times 28$, 1955

89. Dark Trees. Ink wash, 16 × 22, 1961

90. Boulder. Ink and sepia wash, $22\frac{1}{2} \times 30\frac{1}{2}$, 1960's

91. Menemsha Pond. Ink wash, $12\frac{3}{4} \times 19\frac{3}{4}$, 1930's

AN AFTERWORD

Late in 1966, Olivia Mitchell, Adolf Dehn's sister, informed me by letter that Adolf had been hospitalized by a very serious illness. To those of us who knew Adolf, the news was particularly shocking, because he had always shown a kind of ageless vigor that seemed invulnerable. It was a vigor of wit, humor, warm sensibility, and a zest for living that had no accommodation for illness, despite his advancing age.

Sadly, Adolf was never able to resume his life in full measure after his illness. His health remained impaired, and with the impairment, accompanying discouragements set in. Yet for all of this, he continued implacably to work and retained to a remarkable degree all those aspects of personality that made him an incomparable companion and friend, and those refinements of his craft that made him an artist of such singular quality.

It was early in 1968 that I first proposed the idea for this book to Adolf. At that time, I anticipated his complete participation in the process of the book, and he was most enthusiastic, although somewhat dubious that the work would be accepted for publication. These were busy months for him. On top of his other activities and the thinking about the book, an invitation had come from Mahonri Young, Director of The Columbus Gallery of Fine Arts, to assemble a large comprehensive retrospective. It was to include Adolf's work in all media, for exhibition first in Ohio and then at other museums about the country.

I was scheduled to sail for Europe at the end of May, 1968. It had been my intention to stop in New York to visit Adolf and Virginia, his wife, and at that time to discuss with them preliminary ideas for the book. We hoped, too, to make a tentative selection of the drawings to be included. His death on May 19, only days before our planned meeting, thus came as an indescribable shock. All the feelings I had experienced at the news of his illness in 1966 returned, but this time with a sense of desperate finality. A very warm, cordial, and intimate friendship of almost thirty years was ended.

With Adolf's death, the enormously complicated task of assembling the works for the exhibition and of selecting drawings for the book fell chiefly upon Virginia. I spent some time upon my return from Europe and again in April, 1969, in assisting her in selecting the drawings, but the schedule of the traveling exhibition caused some delay. A number of first-rate drawings were included in the retrospective, and Virginia and I wanted these in the book as well.

Adolf Dehn never knew that the publication of his drawings would be assured, since the University of Missouri Press did not act formally to accept the book until July, 1968. Its publication now stands as a memorial to him as an outstanding American artist of the twentieth century, and I am gratified that I was privileged to help in honoring an extra-ordinary artist, a marvelous human being, and a profoundly cherished friend.

Fred Shane

Columbia, Missouri

September, 1970